Improving Made Easy
For Guitar, Bass and Ukulele,
2nd Edition

by Jason Gastrich

Published on September 19, 2023

ISBN (electronic): 978-1-990576-47-8

ISBN (paperback): 978-1-990576-48-5

Dear musician,

No matter which guitar or ukulele you play my system will help you create music in any key. Write your own solos, bridges, hooks, licks and bass lines. If you don't know which key your song is in, you can find it by matching tones (and using the process of elimination) on the page called The Major Keys. Once you know the key, find the corresponding key page to write the rest of your song. Every note on the key page is an option for you to use.

Another way musicians enjoy my system is by playing improvisational music with their favorite songs. Play an audio file and find the key it's in. If need be you can match tones with the notes on The Major Keys page. When you find the right key, turn to the appropriate key page and use the numerical system to find the right notes on the fret board.

Some musicians will use this book to play with other musicians. To jam with someone else all you need to know is the key they're playing in. If the other musician doesn't know the key simply follow the instructions above and find it, then use the corresponding key page. You're instantly able to jam with other musicians.

No matter what your skill level is this system will take you to the next level. Create beautiful music as you play notes up and down the fret board by number like using tabs (tablature). Avoid playing sour notes by accident because you see all your note options by number and it doesn't get much easier than this.

Sincerely,

Jason Gastrich
Instruments teacher
alohamusiclessons.com

Tips for Finding the Key of a Song

1. Tune your guitar and match tones with the song by plucking different notes on your fret board
2. Try listening for and matching the melody or bass notes first because they're usually loudest and prominent
3. Pluck notes next to the fretted note you think is in the song and confirm whether they harmonize or not (many times one will and one won't)
4. Try playing those notes along with the song and confirm or deny them
5. Using the Fret Board sheet and determine the names of the notes that you hear in the song and write them somewhere
6. Find six or seven notes, then use one of the Major Keys sheets (either the one with sharps or flats) to find which key those notes fit in
7. When you try to match tones, some notes will harmonize with the song (which means they're in the key) and others will sound horrible (which means they're not in the key)
8. Remember how every sharp and flat note has two names (e.g. A# and Bb are the same note, D# and Eb are the same note, etc.)
9. Although it isn't scientific and can't be relied on about 80% of the time the first note or chord in the song is also the name of the song's key, so you can always start there

Tips for Creating Great Music

1. Use the four main lead techniques: sliding, bending, hammering and pull-offs

2. Start on one string and try to memorize and play the fret numbers on it for that particular key

3. Alternate the lengths of the notes (e.g. play some half notes, quarter notes, eighth notes, etc.)

4. Avoid playing all of the notes on the down beat and try playing some staccato notes on the upbeat, the downbeat and in between

5. Fill the spaces in a measure (or a few measures) with notes

6. Remember that pausing and making some time for silence is important

7. Identify when similar fret numbers occur on multiple strings and play them on those strings

8. Attempt to find and play the voice melody notes and play before, with or a the vocals with the same notes

9. If you play a sour note that isn't in the right key, identify its fret number and avoid it for the rest of the song

The Major (and Relative Minor) Keys

A (F#m)	A B C# D E F# G#
A# (Gm)	A A# C D D# F G
B (G#m)	A# B C# D# E F# G#
C (Am)	A B C D E F G
C# (A#m)	A# C C# D# F F# G#
D (Bm)	A B C# D E F# G
D# (Cm)	A# C D D# F G G#
E (C#m)	A B C# D# E F# G#
F (Dm)	A A# C D E F G
F# (D#m)	A# B C# D# F F# G#
G (Em)	A B C D E F# G
G# (Fm)	A# C C# D# F G G#

* This key sheet is for naturals and sharps.

Note: When a minor key is used the minor key note is emphasized over its relative major key counterpart even though it's the same key.

The Major (and Relative Minor) Keys

A (Gbm)	A B Db D E Gb Ab
Bb (Gm)	A Bb C D Eb F G
B (Abm)	Ab Bb B Db Eb E Gb
C (Am)	A B C D E F G
Db (Bbm)	Ab Bb C Db Eb F Gb
D (Bm)	A B Db D E Gb G
Eb (Cm)	Ab Bb C D Eb F G
E (Dbm)	A B Db Eb E Gb Ab
F (Dm)	A Bb C D E F G
Gb (Ebm)	Ab Bb B Db Eb F Gb
G (Em)	A B C D E Gb G
Ab (Fm)	Ab Bb C Db Eb F G

* This key sheet is for naturals and flats.

Note: When a minor key is used the minor key note is emphasized over its relative major key counterpart even though it's the same key.

The Guitar and Bass Fretboards

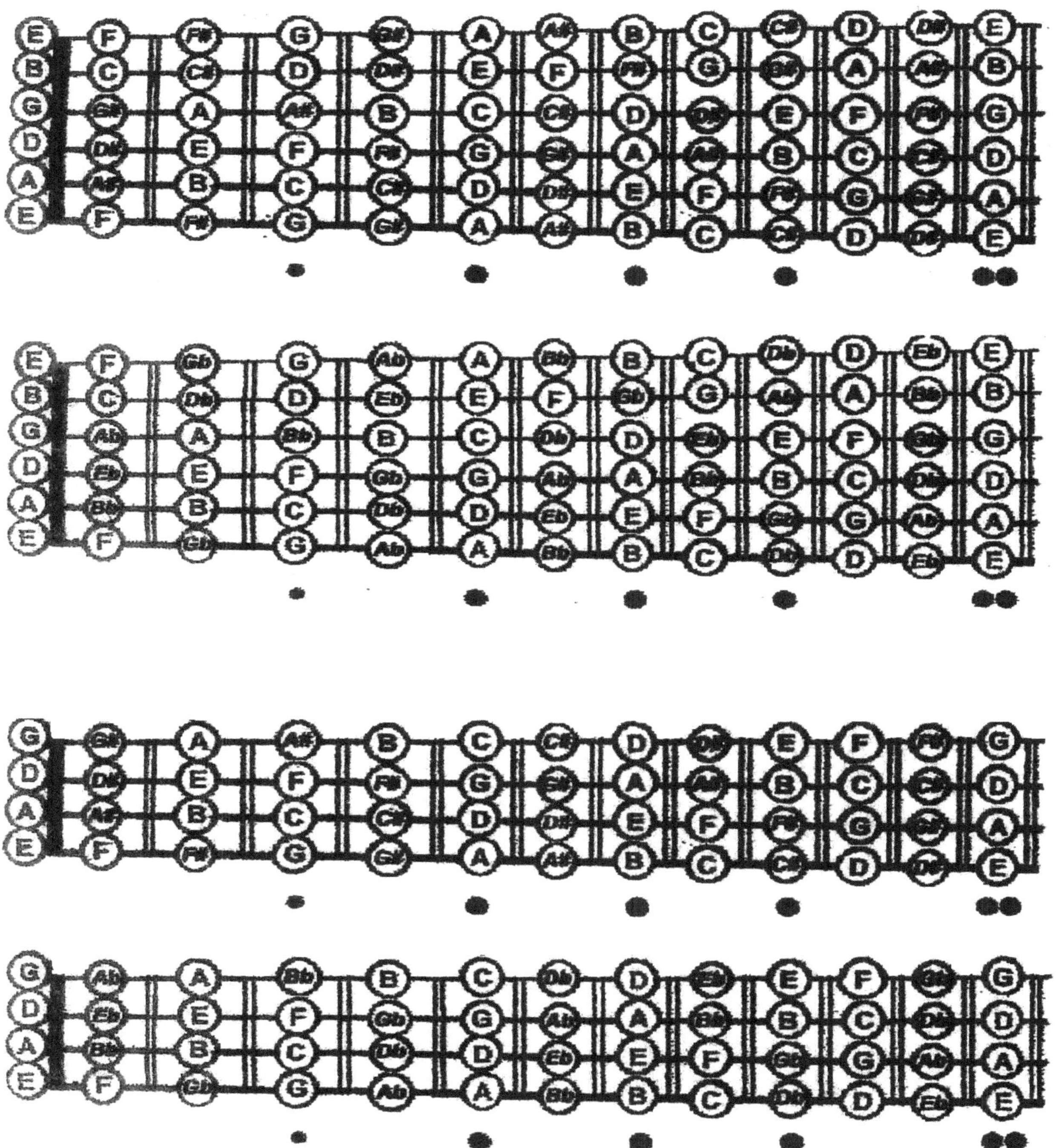

The Key of A

E - 0 , 2 , 4 , 5 , 7 , 9 , 10 , 12 , 14 , 16 , 17 , 19 , 21 , 22 , 24

B - 0 , 2 , 3 , 5 , 7 , 9 , 10 , 12 , 14 , 15 , 17 , 19 , 21 , 22 , 24

G - 1 , 2 , 4 , 6 , 7 , 9 , 11 , 13 , 14 , 16 , 18 , 19 , 21 , 23

D - 0 , 2 , 4 , 6 , 7 , 9 , 11 , 12 , 14 , 16 , 18 , 19 , 21 , 23 , 24

A - 0 , 2 , 4 , 5 , 7 , 9 , 11 , 12 , 14 , 16 , 17 , 19 , 21 , 23 , 24

E - 0 , 2 , 4 , 5 , 7 , 9 , 10 , 12 , 14 , 16 , 17 , 19 , 21 , 22 , 24

Note: F#m is the relative minor key of A major.

The Key of A# or Bb

E – 1 , 3 , 5 , 6 , 8 , 10 , 11 , 13 , 15 , 17 , 18 , 20 , 22 , 23

B – 1 , 3 , 4 , 6 , 8 , 10 , 11 , 13 , 15 , 16 , 18 , 20 , 22 , 23

G – 0 , 2 , 3 , 5 , 7 , 8 , 10 , 12 , 14 , 15 , 17 , 19 , 20 , 22 , 24

D – 0 , 1 , 3 , 5 , 7 , 8 , 10 , 12 , 13 , 15 , 17 , 19 , 20 , 22 , 24

A – 0 , 1 , 3 , 5 , 6 , 8 , 10 , 12 , 13 , 15 , 17 , 18 , 20 , 22 , 24

E – 1 , 3 , 5 , 6 , 8 , 10 , 11 , 13 , 15 , 17 , 18 , 20 , 22 , 23

Note: Gm is the relative minor key of A# and Bb major.

The Key of B

E - 0 , 2 , 4 , 6 , 7 , 9 , 11 , 12 , 14 , 16 , 18 , 19 , 21 , 23 , 24

B - 0 , 2 , 4 , 5 , 7 , 9 , 11 , 12 , 14 , 16 , 17 , 19 , 21 , 23 , 24

G - 1 , 3 , 4 , 6 , 8 , 9 , 11 , 13 , 15 , 16 , 18 , 20 , 21 , 23

D - 1 , 2 , 4 , 6 , 8 , 9 , 11 , 13 , 14 , 16 , 18 , 20 , 21 , 23

A - 1 , 2 , 4 , 6 , 7 , 9 , 11 , 13 , 14 , 16 , 18 , 19 , 21 , 23

E - 0 , 2 , 4 , 6 , 7 , 9 , 11 , 12 , 14 , 16 , 18 , 19 , 21 , 23

Note: G#m is the relative minor key of B major.

The Key of C

E - 0 , 1 , 3 , 5 , 7 , 8 , 10 , 12 , 13 , 15 , 17 , 19 , 20 , 22 , 24

B - 0 , 1 , 3 , 5 , 6 , 8 , 10 , 12 , 13 , 15 , 17 , 18 , 20 , 22 , 24

G - 0 , 2 , 4 , 5 , 7 , 9 , 10 , 12 , 14 , 16 , 17 , 19 , 21 , 22 , 24

D - 0 , 2 , 3 , 5 , 7 , 9 , 10 , 12 , 14 , 15 , 17 , 19 , 21 , 22 , 24

A - 0 , 2 , 3 , 5 , 7 , 8 , 10 , 12 , 14 , 15 , 17 , 19 , 20 , 22 , 24

E - 0 , 1 , 3 , 5 , 7 , 8 , 10 , 12 , 13 , 15 , 17 , 19 , 20 , 22 , 24

Note: Am is the relative minor key of C major.

The Key of C# or Db

E - 1 , 2 , 4 , 6 , 8 , 9 , 11 , 13 , 14 , 16 , 18 , 20 , 21 , 23

B - 1 , 2 , 4 , 6 , 7 , 9 , 11 , 13 , 14 , 16 , 18 , 19 , 21 , 23

G - 1 , 3 , 5 , 6 , 8 , 10 , 11 , 13 , 15 , 17 , 18 , 20 , 22 , 23

D - 1 , 3 , 4 , 6 , 8 , 10 , 11 , 13 , 15 , 16 , 18 , 20 , 22 , 23

A - 1 , 3 , 4 , 6 , 8 , 9 , 11 , 13 , 15 , 16 , 18 , 20 , 21 , 23

E - 1 , 2 , 4 , 6 , 8 , 9 , 11 , 13 , 14 , 16 , 18 , 20 , 21 , 23

Note: A#m is the relative minor key of C# and Db major.

The Key of D

E - 0 , 2 , 3 , 5 , 7 , 9 , 10 , 12 , 14 , 15 , 17 , 19 , 21 , 22 , 24

B - 0 , 2 , 3 , 5 , 7 , 8 , 10 , 12 , 14 , 15 , 17 , 19 , 20 , 22 , 24

G - 0 , 2 , 4 , 6 , 7 , 9 , 11 , 12 , 14 , 16 , 18 , 19 , 21 , 22 , 24

D - 0 , 2 , 4 , 5 , 7 , 9 , 11 , 12 , 14 , 16 , 17 , 19 , 21 , 23

A - 0 , 2 , 4 , 5 , 7 , 9 , 10 , 12 , 14 , 16 , 17 , 19 , 21 , 22 , 24

E - 0 , 2 , 3 , 5 , 7 , 9 , 10 , 12 , 14 , 15 , 17 , 19 , 21 , 22 , 24

Note: Bm is the relative minor key of D major.

The Key of D# or Eb

E – 1 , 3 , 4 , 6 , 8 , 10 , 11 , 13 , 15 , 16 , 18 , 20 , 22 , 23

B – 1 , 3 , 4 , 6 , 8 , 9 , 11 , 13 , 15 , 16 , 18 , 20 , 21 , 23

G – 0 , 1 , 3 , 5 , 7 , 8 , 10 , 12 , 13 , 15 , 17 , 19 , 20 , 22 , 24

D – 0 , 1 , 3 , 5 , 6 , 8 , 10 , 12 , 13 , 15 , 17 , 18 , 20 , 22 , 24

A – 1 , 3 , 5 , 6 , 8 , 10 , 11 , 13 , 15 , 17 , 18 , 20 , 22 , 23

E – 1 , 3 , 4 , 6 , 8 , 10 , 11 , 13 , 15 , 16 , 18 , 20 , 22 , 23

Note: Cm is the relative minor key of D# and Eb major.

The Key of E

E - 0 , 2 , 4 , 5 , 7 , 9 , 11 , 12 , 14 , 16 , 17 , 19 , 21, 23 , 24

B - 0 , 2 , 4 , 5 , 7 , 9 , 10 , 12 , 14 , 16 , 17 , 19 , 21 , 22 , 24

G - 1 , 2 , 4 , 6 , 8 , 9 , 11 , 13 , 14 , 16 , 18 , 20 , 21 , 23

D - 1 , 2 , 4 , 6 , 7 , 9 , 11 , 13 , 14 , 16 , 18 , 19 , 21 , 23

A - 0 , 2 , 4 , 6 , 7 , 9 , 11 , 12 , 14 , 16 , 18 , 19 , 21 , 23

E - 0 , 2 , 4 , 5 , 7 , 9 , 11 , 12 , 14 , 16 , 17 , 19 , 21 , 23 , 24

Note: C#m is the relative minor key of E major.

The Key of F

E - 0 , 1 , 3 , 5 , 6 , 8 , 10 , 12 , 13 , 15 , 17 , 18 , 20 , 22 , 23

B - 1 , 3 , 5 , 6 , 8 , 10 , 11 , 13 , 15 , 17 , 18 , 20 , 22 , 23

G - 0 , 2 , 3 , 5 , 7 , 9 , 10 , 12 , 14 , 15 , 17 , 19 , 21 , 22 , 24

D - 0 , 2 , 3 , 5 , 7 , 8 , 10 , 12 , 14 , 15 , 17 , 19 , 20 , 22 , 24

A - 0 , 1 , 3 , 5 , 7 , 8 , 10 , 12 , 13 , 15 , 17 , 19 , 20 , 22 , 24

E - 0 , 1 , 3 , 5 , 6 , 8 , 10 , 12 , 13 , 15 , 17 , 18 , 20 , 22 , 23

Note: Dm is the relative minor key of F major.

The Key of F# or Gb

E – 1 , 2 , 4 , 6 , 7 , 9 , 11 , 13 , 14 , 16 , 18 , 19 , 21 , 23

B – 0 , 2 , 4 , 6 , 7 , 9 , 11 , 12 , 14 , 16 , 18 , 19 , 21 , 23

G – 1 , 3 , 4 , 6 , 8 , 10 , 11 , 13 , 15 , 16 , 18 , 20 , 21 , 23

D – 1 , 3 , 4 , 6 , 8 , 9 , 11 , 13 , 15 , 16 , 18 , 20 , 21 , 23

A – 1 , 2 , 4 , 6 , 8 , 9 , 11 , 13 , 14 , 16 , 18 , 20 , 21 , 23

E – 1 , 2 , 4 , 6 , 7 , 9 , 11 , 13 , 14 , 16 , 18 , 19 , 21 , 23

Note: D#m is the relative minor key of F# and Gb major.

The Key of G

E - 0 , 2 , 3 , 5 , 7 , 8 , 10 , 12 , 14 , 15 , 17 , 19 , 20 , 22 , 24

B - 0 , 1 , 3 , 5 , 7 , 8 , 10 , 12 , 13 , 15 , 17 , 19 , 20 , 22 , 24

G - 0 , 2 , 4 , 5 , 7 , 9 , 11 , 12 , 14 , 16 , 17 , 19 , 21 , 23 , 24

D - 0 , 2 , 4 , 5 , 7 , 9 , 10 , 12 , 14 , 16 , 17 , 19 , 21 , 22 , 24

A - 0 , 2 , 3 , 5 , 7 , 9 , 10 , 12 , 14 , 15 , 17 , 19 , 21 , 22 , 24

E - 0 , 2 , 3 , 5 , 7 , 8 , 10 , 12 , 14 , 15 , 17 , 19 , 20 , 22 , 24

Note: Em is the relative minor key of G major.

The Key of G# or Ab

E - 1 , 3 , 4 , 6 , 8 , 9 , 11 , 13 , 15 , 16 , 18 , 20 , 21 , 23

B - 1 , 2 , 4 , 6 , 8 , 9 , 11 , 13 , 14 , 16 , 18 , 20 , 21 , 23

G - 0 , 1 , 3 , 5 , 6 , 8 , 10 , 12 , 13 , 15 , 17 , 18 , 20 , 22 , 24

D - 1 , 3 , 5 , 6 , 8 , 10 , 11 , 13 , 15 , 17 , 18 , 20 , 22 , 23

A - 1 , 3 , 4 , 6 , 8 , 10 , 11 , 13 , 15 , 16 , 18 , 20 , 22 , 23

E - 1 , 3 , 4 , 6 , 8 , 9 , 11 , 13 , 15 , 16 , 18 , 20 , 21 , 23

Note: Fm is the relative minor key of G# and Ab major.

The Ukulele Fretboard

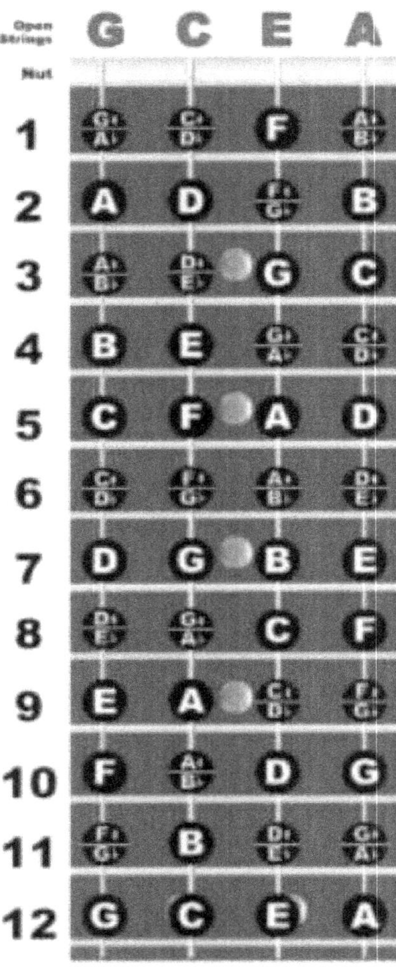

The Key of A

G - 1 , 2 , 4 , 6 , 7 , 9 , 11 , 13 , 14 , 16

C - 1 , 2 , 4 , 6 , 8 , 9 , 11 , 12 , 14 , 16

E - 0 , 2 , 4 , 5 , 7 , 9 , 10 , 12 , 14 , 16 , 17

A - 0 , 2 , 4 , 5 , 7 , 9 , 11 , 12 , 14 , 16 , 17

Note: F#m is the relative minor key of A major.

The Key of A# or Bb

G - 0 , 2 , 3 , 5 , 7 , 8 , 10 , 12 , 14 , 15 , 17

C - 0 , 2 , 3 , 5 , 7 , 9 , 10 , 12 , 14 , 15 , 17

E - 1 , 3 , 5 , 6 , 8 , 10 , 11 , 13 , 15 , 17

A - 0 , 1 , 3 , 5 , 6 , 8 , 10 , 12 , 13 , 15 , 17

Note: F#m is the relative minor key of A major.

The Key of B

G - 1 , 3 , 4 , 6 , 8 , 9 , 11 , 13 , 15 , 16

C - 1 , 3 , 4 , 6 , 8 , 10 , 11 , 13 , 15 , 16

E - 0 , 2 , 4 , 6 , 7 , 9 , 11 , 12 , 14 , 16

A - 1 , 2 , 4 , 6 , 7 , 9 , 11 , 13 , 14 , 16

Note: G#m is the relative minor key of B major.

The Key of C

G - 0 , 2 , 4 , 5 , 7 , 9 , 10 , 12 , 14 , 16 , 17

C - 0 , 2 , 4 , 5 , 7 , 9 , 11 , 12 , 14 , 16 , 17

E - 0 , 1 , 3 , 5 , 7 , 8 , 10 , 12 , 13 , 15 , 16

A - 0 , 2 , 3 , 5 , 7 , 8 , 10 , 12 , 14 , 15 , 17

Note: Am is the relative minor key of C major.

The Key of C# or Db

G - 1 , 3 , 5 , 6 , 8 , 10 , 11 , 13 , 15 , 17

C - 0 , 1 , 3 , 5 , 6 , 8 , 10 , 12 , 13 , 15 , 17

E - 1 , 2 , 4 , 6 , 8 , 9 , 11 , 13 , 14 , 16

A - 1 , 3 , 4 , 6 , 8 , 9 , 11 , 13 , 15 , 16

Note: A#m is the relative minor key of C# and Db major.

The Key of D

G - 0 , 2 , 4 , 6 , 7 , 9 , 11 , 12 , 14 , 16

C - 1 , 2 , 4 , 6 , 7 , 9 , 11 , 13 , 14 , 16

E - 0 , 2 , 3 , 5 , 7 , 9 , 10 , 12 , 14 , 15 , 17

A - 0 , 2 , 4 , 5 , 7 , 9 , 10 , 12 , 14 , 16 , 17

Note: Bm is the relative minor key of D major.

The Key of D# or Eb

G - 0 , 1 , 3 , 5 , 7 , 8 , 10 , 12 , 13 , 15 , 17

C - 0 , 2 , 3 , 5 , 7 , 8 , 10 , 12 , 14 , 15 , 17

E - 1 , 3 , 4 , 6 , 8 , 10 , 11 , 13 , 15 , 16

A - 1 , 3 , 5 , 6 , 8 , 10 , 11 , 13 , 15 , 17

Note: Cm is the relative minor key of D# and Eb major.

The Key of E

G - 0 , 2 , 3 , 5 , 7 , 8 , 10 , 12 , 14 , 15 , 17

C - 1 , 3 , 4 , 6 , 8 , 9 , 11 , 13 , 15 , 16

E - 0 , 2 , 4 , 5 , 7 , 9 , 11 , 12 , 14 , 16 , 17

A - 0 , 2 , 4 , 6 , 7 , 9 , 11 , 12 , 14 , 16

Note: C#m is the relative minor key of E major.

The Key of F

G - 0 , 2 , 3 , 5 , 7 , 9 , 10 , 12 , 14 , 15 , 17

C - 0 , 2 , 4 , 5 , 7 , 9 , 10 , 12 , 14 , 16 , 17

E - 0 , 1 , 3 , 5 , 6 , 8 , 10 , 12 , 13 , 15 , 17

A - 0 , 1 , 3 , 5 , 7 , 8 , 10 , 12 , 13 , 15 , 17

Note: Dm is the relative minor key of F major.

The Key of F# and Gb

G - 1 , 3 , 4 , 6 , 8 , 10 , 11 , 13 , 15

C - 1 , 3 , 5 , 6 , 8 , 10 , 11 , 13 , 15

E - 1 , 2 , 4 , 6 , 7 , 9 , 11 , 13 , 14

A - 1 , 2 , 4 , 6 , 8 , 9 , 11 , 13 , 14

Note: D#m is the relative minor key of F# and Gb major.

The Key of G

G - 0 , 2 , 4 , 5 , 7 , 9 , 11 , 12 , 14

C - 0 , 2 , 4 , 6 , 7 , 9 , 11 , 12 , 14

E - 0 , 2 , 3 , 5 , 7 , 8 , 10 , 12 , 14 , 15

A - 0 , 2 , 3 , 5 , 7 , 9 , 10 , 12 , 14 , 15

Note: Em is the relative minor key of G major.

The Key of G# or Eb

G - 0 , 1 , 3 , 5 , 6 , 8 , 10 , 12 , 13 , 15

C - 0 , 1 , 3 , 5 , 7 , 8 , 10 , 12 , 13 , 15

E - 1 , 3 , 4 , 6 , 8 , 9 , 11 , 13 , 15

A - 1 , 3 , 4 , 6 , 8 , 10 , 11 , 13 , 15

Note: Fm is the relative minor key of G# or Ab major.

www.ingramcontent.com/pod-product-compliance
Lightning Source LLC
Chambersburg PA
CBHW080752070726
47595CB00017B/4116